THE
CULTURED
COCKTAIL

SKOL

SALUD

PROSIT

CHEERS

L'CHAIM

BOTTOMS UP

NA ZDOROVIA

THE CULTURED COCKTAIL

150 Classic Drinks from the Jazz Age to the Space Age {with delicious variations for the designated driver}

BY *Katharine Williams*

ILLUSTRATIONS BY *Susan Gross*

CLARKSON POTTER/PUBLISHERS

NEW YORK

Dedicated to the memory of
Al Williams, my beloved husband,
who taught me about food, drink, life, and love

PUBLISHED BY CLARKSON N. POTTER, INC., 201 EAST 50TH STREET, NEW YORK, NEW YORK 10022. MEMBER OF THE CROWN PUBLISHING GROUP.

RANDOM HOUSE, INC. NEW YORK, TORONTO, LONDON, SYDNEY, AUCKLAND

CLARKSON N. POTTER, POTTER, AND COLOPHON ARE TRADEMARKS OF CLARKSON N. POTTER, INC.

MANUFACTURED IN CHINA

LIBRARY OF CONGRESS CATALOGING-IN-PUBLICATION DATA
WILLIAMS, KATHARINE.
THE CULTURED COCKTAIL : 150 DRINKS FROM THE JAZZ AGE TO THE SPACE AGE/BY KATHARINE WILLIAMS:
ILLUSTRATIONS BY SUSAN GROSS.
P.CM.
INCLUDES INDEX
1. COCKTAILS. 2. BARTENDING—HANDBOOKS, MANUALS, ETC.   I. TITLE
TX951.W53 1996
641.8'74—DC20   95-22066
                                                        CIP
ISBN 0-517-70208-8

10   9   8   7   6   5   4   3

F L Y
PRODUCTIONS

Contents

INTRODUCTION

Imagine the fortuitous moment, ages and ages ago, when one of our early ancestors came upon a bubbling bunch of wild berries lying under a tree, tentatively touched a finger to the fermenting mash, tasted it, and smiled. The rest is winery! Fossilized grape skins found in Neolithic caves and detailed instructions for the distillation of wheat written in hieroglyphics are documented proof of our ancient attachment to the "water of life." The ritual of marking important moments with a raised cup, a toast to good health, and a clinking of glasses is a tradition handed down through time. ❡Taking this long view, the cocktail is still in its infancy. The golden age was undoubtedly the Roaring Twenties of this century, when many of the cocktails we think of as classics were invented to mask the flavor of bootleg liquor. If the 1920s was the golden age, then the 1990s marks a renaissance, with traditional favorites, modern cocktails, and "smart drinks" — delicious alcohol-free

COLLINS (10 - 14 ounces)

CULTURED
COCKTAIL
GLASSES

HIGHBALL (8 - 10 ounces)

OLD-FASHIONED (6 - 10 ounces)

SHOT (1 1/2 - 2 ounces)

SOUR (4 - 6 ounces)

CHAMPAGNE FLUTE (6 - 8 ounces)

RED WINE (8 - 10 ounces)

WHITE WINE (4 - 6 ounces)

COCKTAIL (3 - 6 ounces)

IRISH COFFEE (8 - 10 ounces)

PUNCH (6 - 8 ounces)

alternatives for designated drivers or nondrinkers — all currently in vogue. ❡To present the perfect cocktail or alcohol-free mixed drink, you need to set up an efficient at-home bar with the proper equipment, glassware, and well-stocked pantry to suit your style of entertaining. To host a successful cocktail party, the glasses on your A list should include: cocktail, collins, highball, sour, shot, champagne flute, and old-fashioned. It helps to have Irish coffee mugs, a punch bowl with a set of punch cups, a large pitcher, and both red and white wineglasses. ❡If dinner parties are more your style, the wineglasses, Irish coffee mugs, large pitcher, and punch bowl setup should be moved to your A list. To serve elegant aperitifs and after-dinner drinks choose champagne flutes, sour glasses, or classic cocktail glasses. Red wine goblets are perfect substitutes for collins, highball, or old-fashioned glasses. ❡A cocktail that is prepared and served with classic accoutrements really does taste better. Essential at-home bar equipment includes a blender, a sixteen-ounce cocktail shaker and strainer, a sixteen-ounce measuring glass, measuring spoons, a measuring cup, and a jigger to mix beautifully balanced drinks, as well as a cork screw, a bottle opener, a can opener, a champagne stopper, a citrus juicer, a sharp paring knife, and an ice bucket with tongs. ❡Stock your pantry and refrigerator with mixers, condiments, and garnishes to shake up a cocktail at the sound of the doorbell. The basic mixers are still and carbonated bottled water, club soda, tonic, cola, ginger ale, tomato juice, and assorted citrus and tropical fruit juices. The basic condiments are sweet flavorings such as grenadine syrup, superfine sugar, coconut cream, and Rose's lime juice; tart tastes such as fresh lemon and lime juices, Angostura, and orange bitters; and to suit the spicy, stock bottles of horseradish, Tabasco, and Worcestershire sauce. The key to preparing perfect alcohol-free versions of classic cocktails is bottled syrups that taste like flavored liqueurs — some people prefer them to the real thing. The syrups are reasonably priced, so it's possible to keep a good selection on hand for a nondrinker. ❡At holiday time, it's wise to have a container of egg substitute in your freezer. The recipes for wonderful concoctions such as eggnog and brandy flip call for raw eggs. For health sake, without sacrificing flavor, I include the egg substitute equivalent when raw eggs are used in the recipe. Egg substitute cannot be whipped to form peaks and therefore cannot be substituted in the Tom & Jerry recipe. ❦No cultured cocktail is complete without its signature garnish. What would a martini be without a green olive? A mint julep without a sprig of mint? A Manhattan without a maraschino cherry? To flavor and decorate a variety of drinks, use green olives, cocktail onions, and maraschino cherries; lemons, limes, oranges, and pineapples; mint, cinnamon, nutmeg, cloves, salt, and black pepper. And perhaps a festive paper umbrella. ❦The perfect at-home bar is a reflection of the host's lifestyle. I always have bottles of vodka, gin, and tequila on hand, with dry white wine and a bottle of champagne usually chilling in my refrigerator. It's not necessary, however, to replicate the Oak Room at the Plaza! Why not find a signature drink and always keep the necessary ingredients around? I love to cook Mexican food, and my friends know that when they dine at my house they'll be served the tartest and most thirst-quenching margarita in Marin County. ❦Whatever your entertaining style, you'll have fun preparing and serving a cultured cocktail in the classic way.

BOCCI BALL

STINGER

SLOE GIN FIZZ

CADIZ

GRASSHOPPER

BRANDY FLIP

BRANDY ALEXANDER

EGGNOG

FLAVORED LIQUEUR

Brandy Alexander. Sidecar. Stinger. Sloe gin fizz. Grasshopper. Just saying the names of these sophisticated flavored-liqueur cocktails suggests *soigné soirées*. ❡ Flavored liqueurs are divided into two distinctive groups: brandies and cordials. Brandy is the product of distilled barrel-aged wine. Most often made from grape wine, rich-tasting brandies are also produced from apple, berry, peach, or apricot wine. Cordials, or sweet liqueurs, are the distilled essences of pungent herbs, ripe fruits, and flavorful nuts, beans, and seeds. ❡ Premier brandy is produced in the French regions of Cognac and Armagnac and is perfection on its own, warmed and fragrant in a snifter, but its flavor is wasted in a cocktail. The best brandy for mixed drinks is domestic grape-wine brandy. ❡ Brandy and cordial cocktails are wonderful served before dinner as an aperitif, or after dinner with dessert and coffee.

AMERICAN BEAUTY

makes two cocktails

1 1/2 ounces brandy
1 1/2 ounces dry vermouth
1 ounce grenadine
1 ounce white crème de menthe
1 ounce orange juice
1 ounce port

In a cocktail shaker, half full of ice cubes, combine all the ingredients except the port. Shake to mix. Strain the mixture into two highball glasses. Float half an ounce of port in each drink. Do not stir.

BETSY ROSS

makes two cocktails

3 ounces brandy
3 ounces port
2 dashes Angostura bitters
2 drops blue Curaçao

In a cocktail shaker, half full of ice cubes, combine all the ingredients. Shake to mix. Strain the mixture into two white wineglasses.

BRANDY ALEXANDER

makes two cocktails

4 ounces brandy
2 ounces crème de cacao
2 ounces heavy cream
Grated nutmeg

In a cocktail shaker, half full of crushed ice, combine all the ingredients except the nutmeg. Shake to mix. Strain into two cocktail glasses. Garnish each drink with grated nutmeg.

DESIGNATED DRIVER BRANDY ALEXANDER: Chill a highball glass. Pour *1 ounce of whole milk* and *1 1/2 tablespoons of chocolate syrup* into the glass. Fill to the top with *soda water*. Stir.

EGGNOG

makes six cocktails

6 eggs (12 ounces egg substitute)
2 teaspoons vanilla extract
3 tablespoons powdered sugar
12 ounces whole milk
12 ounces brandy
Grated nutmeg

In a large mixing bowl, combine the eggs, vanilla, and sugar. Whisk until the mixture thickens and the sugar dissolves. Add the milk and the brandy. Stir. Cover and chill for two hours. Transfer the eggnog to a punch bowl. Garnish each punch cup with grated nutmeg.

STINGER

makes two cocktails

3 ounces brandy
1 ounce white crème de menthe

In a cocktail shaker, half full of ice cubes, combine the ingredients. Shake to mix. Strain the mixture into two cocktail glasses.

DESIGNATED DRIVER STINGER: Pour *1 ounce of crème de menthe syrup* into a collins glass. Fill to the top with *crushed ice* and *soda water*. Stir.

TOM & JERRY

makes two cocktails

2 eggs, separated
1/4 teaspoon baking soda
2 teaspoons sugar
1 1/2 ounces brandy
1 1/2 ounces rum
10 ounces whole milk, heated
Grated nutmeg

Warm two Irish coffee mugs. In a mixing bowl, whisk the egg whites into soft peaks. In a second bowl, whisk the yolks to a froth. Fold the whites into the yolks. Add the baking soda and the sugar. Whisk the mixture until it stiffens. Fold in the brandy and the rum. Pour the mixture into the mugs. Fill to the top with hot milk. Stir. Garnish each drink with a sprinkle of grated nutmeg.

SIDECAR

makes two cocktails

3 ounces brandy
2 ounces triple sec
2 ounces lemon juice

In a cocktail shaker, half full of ice cubes, combine all the ingredients. Shake to mix. Strain the mixture into two cocktail glasses.

DESIGNATED DRIVER SIDECAR: Pour *1/2 an ounce of lemon juice* and *1 tablespoon of superfine sugar* into a collins glass, half full of ice cubes. Fill with *soda water.* Stir gently.

BRANDY FLIP

makes two cocktails

2 eggs (4 ounces egg substitute)
2 teaspoons superfine sugar
3 ounces brandy
1 ounce heavy cream
Grated nutmeg

In a cocktail shaker, half full of ice cubes, combine all the ingredients except the grated nutmeg. Shake to mix. Strain the mixture into two sour glasses. Garnish each drink with a sprinkle of grated nutmeg.

Cordials

JACK ROSE

makes two cocktails

3 ounces applejack
1 1/2 ounces lemon juice
1 ounce grenadine

In a cocktail shaker, half full of ice cubes, combine all the ingredients. Shake to mix. Strain the mixture into two cocktail glasses.

GOLD CADILLAC

makes two cocktails

4 ounces Galliano
2 ounces white crème de menthe
2 ounces heavy cream

In a cocktail shaker, half full of ice cubes, combine all the ingredients. Shake to mix. Strain the mixture into two cocktail glasses.

KISS ME QUICK

m a k e s   t w o   c o c k t a i l s

4 ounces Pernod
2 teaspoons Cointreau
3 drops Angostura bitters
12 ounces soda water

In a cocktail shaker, half full of ice cubes, combine all the ingredients except the soda water. Shake to mix. Strain into two highball glasses. Fill with soda water. Stir.

DESIGNATED DRIVER KISS ME QUICK: Chill a highball glass. Pour *1/2 an ounce of anisette syrup, 3 ounces of orange juice,* and *1 drop of Angostura bitters* into the glass. Fill with *soda water* and *ice cubes*. Stir.

FRIAR TUCK

m a k e s   t w o   c o c k t a i l s

4 ounces Frangelico
4 ounces lemon juice
2 teaspoons grenadine
2 orange slices

In a cocktail shaker, half full of ice cubes, combine all the ingredients except the orange slices. Shake. Strain into two cocktail glasses. Garnish with orange slices.

DESIGNATED DRIVER FRIAR TUCK: Chill an old-fashioned glass. Pour *1/2 ounce of hazelnut syrup, 1 ounce of lemon juice,* and *1 teaspoon of grenadine* into the glass. Fill with *soda water* and *ice*. Garnish with an *orange slice*.

BOCCI BALL

m a k e s   t w o   c o c k t a i l s

4 ounces amaretto
12 ounces orange juice
2 orange twists

Chill two highball glasses. Pour two ounces of amaretto and six ounces of orange juice into each glass, half full of ice cubes. Stir. Garnish each with an orange twist.

DESIGNATED DRIVER BOCCI BALL: Chill a highball glass. Pour *1 ounce of almond syrup* into the glass. Fill to the top with *orange juice* and *ice cubes*. Stir to mix.

CADIZ

m a k e s   t w o   c o c k t a i l s

2 ounces black raspberry liqueur
2 ounces Amontillado sherry
1 ounce triple sec
1 ounce heavy cream

Chill two old-fashioned glasses. In a cocktail shaker, half full of crushed ice, combine all the ingredients. Shake to mix. Strain the mixture into the glasses.

GRASSHOPPER

makes two cocktails

2 ounces crème de menthe
2 ounces crème de cacao
2 ounces heavy cream

In a cocktail shaker, half full of ice cubes, combine all the ingredients. Shake to mix. Strain the mixture into two cocktail glasses. Serve with cocktail straws. **DESIGNATED DRIVER GRASSHOPPER:** Chill a highball glass. Pour *1 ounce of whole milk* and *1 1/2 tablespoons of crème de menthe syrup* into the glass. Fill to the top with *soda water*. Stir gently.

LONDON FOG

makes two cocktails

1 ounce anisette
1 ounce white crème de menthe
2 dashes Angostura bitters

In a cocktail shaker, combine all the ingredients. Shake to mix. Place the mixture and two cocktail glasses in the refrigerator to chill for one hour. Strain the mixture into the glasses.

SLOE GIN FIZZ

makes two cocktails

2 ounces sloe gin
2 ounces gin
1 ounce lemon juice
6 ounces soda water
2 lemon slices

In a cocktail shaker, half full of ice cubes, combine all the ingredients except the soda water and the lemon slices. Shake to mix. Strain the mixture into two sour glasses. Fill to the top with soda water. Garnish each drink with a slice of lemon.

DESIGNATED DRIVER SLOE GIN FIZZ: In a cocktail shaker, a quarter full of ice cubes, combine *4 ounces of cherry juice* and *1 ounce of almond syrup*. Shake to mix. Strain the mixture into a sour glass. Fill to the top with *soda water*. Garnish with a *lemon slice*.

GIN

Legend has it that excessive gin drinking was what caused Prohibition in America. Notorious gin, the "Mother of Ruin," is the main ingredient in the queen of cocktails, the martini. Brewed for the first time some three hundred years ago in Holland, gin is a distillation of juniper berries and an assortment of other aromatic herbs. ¶The British claim credit for perfecting the crisp, dry, pungently flavored liquid, but Americans — supposedly, New Yorkers — concocted the marvelous martini. Invented at the turn of the century by the bartender at the Knickerbocker Hotel in midtown Manhattan, the first martini was stirred, not shaken (apologies to 007), by Martini di Arma di Taggia and served to none other than John D. Rockefeller. Playing second fiddle to the martini, but still holding their own, are the classic gin cocktails: the Gibson, the gimlet, the pink lady, the Tom Collins, and the Singapore sling.

GIN FIZZ

SINGAPORE SLING

GIBSON

MARTINI

GIN & TONIC

TOM COLLINS

TOM COLLINS

makes two cocktails

4 ounces gin
3 ounces lemon juice
2 teaspoons superfine sugar
10 ounces soda water
2 maraschino cherries

In a cocktail shaker, half full of ice cubes, combine all the ingredients except the soda water and the cherries. Shake to mix. Strain the mixture into two collins glasses. Fill to the top with soda water and ice cubes. Garnish each drink with a maraschino cherry.

NEGRONI

makes two cocktails

2 ounces gin
2 ounces Campari
2 ounces sweet vermouth
2 lemon twists

Chill two cocktail glasses. In a mixing glass, half full of ice cubes, combine all the ingredients except the lemon twists. Stir to mix. Strain the mixture into the glasses. Garnish each drink with a twist of lemon.

PINK LADY

makes two cocktails

2 ounces gin
1 ounce grenadine
3 ounces heavy cream

Chill two cocktail glasses. In a cocktail shaker, half full of crushed ice, combine all the ingredients. Shake to mix. Strain the mixture into the glasses.

GIN & TONIC

makes two cocktails

4 ounces gin
16 ounces tonic water
2 lime wedges

Chill two collins glasses. Pour two ounces of gin into each glass. Fill to the top with tonic water and ice cubes. Garnish each drink with a lime wedge.

GIBSON

4 ounces gin
1 ounce dry vermouth
2 cocktail onions

In a mixing glass, half full of ice cubes, combine the ingredients except the cocktail onions. Stir to mix. Strain the mixture into two cocktail glasses. Garnish each drink with a cocktail onion.

GIMLET

4 ounces gin
1 ounce Rose's lime juice
2 lime slices

Chill two cocktail glasses. In a mixing glass, half full of ice cubes, combine the ingredients except the lime slices. Stir to mix. Strain the mixture into the glasses. Garnish each drink with a slice of lime.

GIN FIZZ

6 ounces gin
3 ounces lemon juice
3 ounces lime juice
2 tablespoons superfine sugar
8 ounces soda water
2 orange slices
2 maraschino cherries

Chill two collins glasses. In a cocktail shaker, half full of ice cubes, combine all the ingredients except the soda water, the orange slices, and the maraschino cherries. Shake to mix. Strain the mixture into the glasses. Fill to the top with soda water. Stir gently. Garnish each drink with a slice of orange and a maraschino cherry.

DESIGNATED DRIVER GIN FIZZ: Chill a collins glass. Pour *1 1/2 ounces of lemon juice, 1 1/2 ounces of lime juice,* and *1 tablespoon of sugar* into the glass. Stir to dissolve the sugar. Fill to the top with *soda water.* Stir. Garnish with an *orange slice* and a *maraschino cherry.*

MARTINI

4 ounces gin
2 teaspoons dry vermouth
2 green olives

Chill two cocktail glasses. In a mixing glass, half full of ice cubes, combine all the ingredients except the olives. Stir gently. Strain the mixture into the glasses. Garnish each drink with an olive, speared on a toothpick.

ORANGE BLOSSOM

2 ounces gin
2 ounces orange juice
1 teaspoon superfine sugar
2 orange slices

Chill two cocktail glasses. In a cocktail shaker, half full of crushed ice, combine all the ingredients except the orange slices. Shake to mix. Strain the mixture into the glasses. Garnish each drink with an orange slice.

SINGAPORE SLING

4 ounces gin
2 ounces cherry brandy
1/2 ounce lime juice
3 dashes Bènèdictine
16 ounces soda water

Chill two collins glasses. In a cocktail shaker, half full of ice cubes, combine all the ingredients except the soda water. Shake to mix. Strain the mixture into the glasses. Fill to the top with soda water and ice cubes. Stir gently.

DESIGNATED DRIVER SINGAPORE SLING:
Chill a collins glass. Pour *2 ounces of cherry juice* and *1/2 an ounce of lime juice* into the glass. Stir gently. Fill to the top with *soda water* and *ice cubes*.

DAIQUIRI

ZOMBIE

PIÑA COLADA

HOT BUTTERED RUM

MAI TAI

RUM

Rum is the signature spirit of the Caribbean. Classic rum cocktails — Cuba libre, banana bliss, beachcomber, piña colada, and planter's punch — wear Torrid Zone name tags to describe their tropical, fruity flavors. Distilled from the juice of pressed sugarcane or fermented from its sticky by-product, molasses, rum is then allowed to mature for at least a year and sometimes as long as sixteen. ¶Rums are as unique as the islands they hail from. Superior, light young rum comes from Puerto Rico. The mature, full-bodied Jamaican dark rum is considered the best of its kind, with straw hats off to the buttery dark rum of Barbados. ¶Rum is strong firewater, usually eighty proof (40 percent alcohol). All of the rum cocktail recipes call for eighty-proof light or dark rum, with the appropriately notable exception of the zombie, which is mixed to trancelike potency with 151 proof rum (75 percent alcohol).

BEACHCOMBER

1 lime wedge
Superfine sugar
3 ounces light rum
2 teaspoons lime juice
2 teaspoons triple sec
2 teaspoons maraschino liqueur

Moisten the rims of two cocktail glasses with the lime wedge. Press the rims into a bowl of superfine sugar to coat. In a cocktail shaker, half full of ice cubes, combine all the remaining ingredients. Shake to mix. Strain the mixture into the glasses.

BETWEEN THE SHEETS

makes two cocktails

2 ounces light rum
2 ounces brandy
2 ounces Cointreau
2 teaspoons lemon juice

In a cocktail shaker, half full of ice cubes, combine all the ingredients. Shake to mix. Strain the mixture into two highball glasses, filled almost to the top with ice cubes.

BANANA BLISS

makes two cocktails

3 ounces light rum
1 ounce banana liqueur
1 ounce orange juice
2 ounces heavy cream
2 dashes grenadine

Chill two cocktail glasses. In a cocktail shaker, half full of ice cubes, combine all the ingredients. Shake to mix. Strain the mixture into the glasses.

DESIGNATED DRIVER BANANA BLISS: Chill a cocktail glass. In a blender, combine *1/2 of a banana, 1 ounce of orange juice, 1 ounce of heavy cream, a dash of grenadine*, and *4 ice cubes*. Blend at high speed for thirty seconds. Pour the blissful smoothie into the glass.

CUBA LIBRE

makes two cocktails

3 ounces light rum
14 ounces cola
2 lime wedges

Chill two highball glasses. Pour an ounce and a half of rum and six ounces of cola into each glass, half full of ice cubes. Stir to mix. Garnish each drink with a lime wedge.

DAIQUIRI

makes two cocktails

4 ounces light rum
2 ounces lime juice
2 teaspoons sugar
2 lime slices

In a cocktail shaker, half full of ice cubes, combine all the ingredients except the lime slices. Shake to mix. Strain the mixture into two cocktail glasses. Garnish each drink with a slice of lime.

GROG

makes two cocktails

4 ounces Jamaican dark rum
2 sugar cubes
1 ounce lemon juice
6 whole cloves
2 cinnamon sticks
2 lemon twists

Warm two Irish coffee mugs. Pour two ounces of Jamaican rum into each mug. Add one sugar cube, half an ounce of lemon juice, three cloves, and a cinnamon stick to each drink. Fill to the top with boiling water. Stir to dissolve the sugar. Garnish each drink with a lemon twist.

DESIGNATED DRIVER GROG: Warm an Irish coffee mug. Place *1 sugar cube, 1/2 an ounce of lemon juice, 3 cloves,* and *1 cinnamon stick* into the mug. Fill to the top with *hibiscus tea.* Stir to dissolve the sugar. Garnish with a *lemon twist.*

MAI TAI

makes two cocktails

6 ounces light rum
1/2 ounce lime juice
2 teaspoons triple sec
2 teaspoons almond syrup
2 teaspoons superfine sugar
2 pineapple slices
2 mint sprigs

In a cocktail shaker, half full of ice cubes, combine all the ingredients except the pineapple and mint. Shake. Strain into two collins glasses, half full of crushed ice. Garnish each with a pineapple slice and a mint sprig.

PRESIDENTE

makes two cocktails

3 ounces light rum
1 ounce dry vermouth
1 ounce Curaçao
2 dashes grenadine

In a cocktail shaker, half full of ice cubes, combine all the ingredients. Shake to mix. Strain the mixture into two highball glasses, half full of ice cubes.

HOT BUTTERED RUM

makes two cocktails

8 ounces apple cider
12 whole cloves
2 cinnamon sticks
1 ounce lemon juice
4 ounces dark rum
2 tablespoons butter

In a nonreactive saucepan, combine all the ingredients except the rum and the butter. Bring to a boil. Pour the mixture into two Irish coffee mugs. Add two ounces of rum to each mug. Stir to mix. Garnish each drink with one tablespoon of butter.

DESIGNATED DRIVER HOT BUTTERED RUM:

In a nonreactive saucepan, combine *8 ounces of apple cider, 6 cloves, 1 cinnamon stick,* and *1/2 an ounce of lemon juice.* Bring to a boil. Pour the mixture into an Irish coffee mug. Garnish with *1 tablespoon of butter.*

PLANTER'S PUNCH

makes two cocktails

4 ounces dark rum
6 ounces orange juice
2 ounces lime juice
2 teaspoons superfine sugar
2 dashes grenadine
12 ounces soda water
2 orange slices
2 maraschino cherries

Chill two collins glasses. In a cocktail shaker, half full of ice cubes, combine all the ingredients except the soda water, orange slices, and maraschino cherries. Shake to mix. Strain the mixture into the glasses. Fill to the top with soda water. Garnish each drink with an orange slice and a maraschino cherry, speared on a toothpick. Serve with cocktail straws.

DESIGNATED DRIVER PLANTER'S PUNCH: Chill a collins glass. In a cocktail shaker, half full of ice cubes, combine *3 ounces of orange juice, 1 ounce of lime juice, 1 teaspoon of superfine sugar,* **and** *1 dash of grenadine.* Shake to mix. Strain into the glass. Fill to the top with *soda water.* Garnish with an *orange slice* and a *maraschino cherry,* speared on a toothpick. Serve with cocktail straws.

PIÑA COLADA

makes two cocktails

4 ounces light rum
4 ounces coconut cream
4 ounces pineapple juice
2 pineapple slices
2 maraschino cherries

Chill two red wineglasses. In a blender, half full of crushed ice, combine all the ingredients except the pineapple slices and the maraschino cherries. Blend at high speed for thirty seconds. Pour the mixture into the glasses. Garnish each drink with a pineapple slice and a maraschino cherry, speared on a toothpick.

DESIGNATED DRIVER PIÑA COLADA: Chill a red wineglass. In a blender, half full of crushed ice, combine *2 ounces of coconut cream* and *4 ounces of pineapple juice.* Blend at high speed for thirty seconds. Pour the mixture into the glass. Garnish with a *pineapple slice* and a *maraschino cherry,* speared on a toothpick.

SCORPION

makes two cocktails

4 ounces dark rum
4 ounces orange juice
2 ounces brandy
1 ounce lemon juice
1/2 ounce almond extract
2 maraschino cherries

Chill two cocktail glasses. In a cocktail shaker, half full of crushed ice, combine all the ingredients except the maraschino cherries. Shake to mix. Strain the mixture into the glasses. Garnish each drink with a maraschino cherry.

DESIGNATED DRIVER SCORPION: Chill a cocktail glass. In a cocktail shaker, half full of crushed ice, combine *5 ounces of orange juice, 1/2 an ounce of lemon juice,* and a *1/4 ounce of almond extract.* Shake to mix. Strain the mixture into the glass. Garnish with a *maraschino cherry.*

ZOMBIE

makes two cocktails

3 ounces dark rum
1 ounce Jamaican rum
1 ounce light rum
2 ounces lime juice
1 ounce pineapple juice
1 ounce orange juice
2 teaspoons superfine sugar
2 teaspoons 151 proof rum
2 orange slices
2 maraschino cherries
2 mint sprigs

Chill two highball glasses. In a blender, combine all the ingredients except the 151 proof rum, the orange slices, the maraschino cherries, and the mint sprigs. Blend at high speed for thirty seconds. Pour the mixture into the glasses. Float one teaspoon of 151 proof rum in each drink. Do not stir. Garnish with an orange slice, a maraschino cherry, and a sprig of mint.

DESIGNATED DRIVER ZOMBIE: Chill a highball glass. Pour *4 ounces of orange juice, 4 ounces of pineapple juice, 1/2 an ounce of lime juice,* and *1 teaspoon of sugar* into the glass. Stir to dissolve the sugar. Garnish with an *orange slice,* a *maraschino cherry,* and a *sprig of mint.*

SCOTCH

Scotch is as welcoming and warm, good-natured and sharp-tongued as the citizens that distill it. Afforded the same respect as a fine Cognac, the brewing and aging of the single-malted barley is a highly sensitive process, calling into play complex environmental conditions. The sweetness of the spring water, the ripeness of the peat, the shape of the still, the provenance of the oak barrel, the length of time the young Scotch is left to age — some say even the salty sea air that surrounds the keg — all influence the flavor. ¶Ninety percent of Highland single-malt Scotch is exported to produce blended Scotch, a combination of several single malts with grain whiskey. Many Scotch-lovers prefer the balanced taste of blended Scotch to the idiosyncratic flavor of single-malt Scotch. ¶All the Scotch cocktails call for blended Scotch except the Scotch mist, a bonny drink with just a wee twist of lemon to brighten the taste.

ROB ROY

FLYING SCOTSMAN

HIGHLAND FLING

RUSTY NAIL

GODFATHER

SCOTCH MIST

RUSTY NAIL

makes two cocktails

4 ounces Scotch
2 ounces Drambuie
2 lemon twists

Chill two old-fashioned glasses. Pour two ounces of Scotch and one ounce of Drambuie into each glass, half full of ice cubes. Stir to mix. Garnish each drink with a twist of lemon.

BLOOD & SAND

makes two cocktails

2 ounces Scotch
1 1/2 ounces cherry brandy
1 1/2 ounces sweet vermouth
1 1/2 ounces orange juice

Chill two cocktail glasses. In a cocktail shaker, half full of ice cubes, combine all the ingredients. Shake to mix. Strain the mixture into the glasses. **DESIGNATED DRIVER BLOOD & SAND:** Chill a cocktail glass. Pour *2 ounces of orange juice* and *1 ounce of cherry juice* into the glass. Stir.

BARBARY COAST

makes two cocktails

2 ounces Scotch
2 ounces light rum
2 ounces gin
2 ounces crème de cacao
2 ounces heavy cream

Chill two cocktail glasses. In a cocktail shaker, half full of ice cubes, combine all the ingredients. Shake to mix. Strain the mixture into the glasses.

BOBBY BURNS

makes two cocktails

2 ounces Scotch
1 1/2 ounces dry vermouth
1 1/2 ounces sweet vermouth
2 dashes Bènèdictine

In a cocktail shaker, half full of ice cubes, combine all the ingredients. Shake to mix. Strain the mixture into two cocktail glasses.

HIGHLAND FLING

makes two cocktails

3 ounces Scotch
2 ounces sweet vermouth
3 dashes orange bitters
2 green olives

Chill two cocktail glasses. In a mixing glass, half full of ice cubes, combine all the ingredients except the green olives. Stir to mix. Pour the mixture into the glasses. Garnish each drink with a green olive.

GODFATHER

makes two cocktails

3 ounces Scotch
1 1/2 ounces amaretto

Chill two old-fashioned glasses. Pour one ounce of Scotch and three-quarters of an ounce of amaretto into two each glass, half full of ice cubes. Stir to mix.

DESIGNATED DRIVER GODFATHER: Chill an old-fashioned glass. Pour *1 ounce of almond syrup* into the glass, half full of ice cubes. Fill to the top with *soda water*. Stir gently.

FLYING SCOTSMAN

makes two cocktails

2 ounces Scotch
2 ounces sweet vermouth
2 teaspoons superfine sugar
2 dashes Angostura bitters

In a cocktail shaker, half full of ice cubes, combine all the ingredients. Shake to mix. Strain the mixture into two old-fashioned glasses, half full of ice cubes.

CAMERON'S KICK

makes two cocktails

1 1/2 ounces Scotch
1 1/2 ounces Irish whiskey
1 ounce lemon juice
2 dashes orange bitters

In a cocktail shaker, half full of ice cubes, combine all the ingredients. Shake to mix. Strain the mixture into two cocktail glasses.

HOPSCOTCH

makes two cocktails

3 ounces Scotch
1 ounce dry vermouth
4 dashes bitters
2 lemon twists

Chill two cocktail glasses. In a cocktail shaker, half full of crushed ice, combine all the ingredients except the lemon twists. Shake to mix. Strain the mixture into the glasses. Garnish each drink with a twist of lemon.

REMSEN COOLER

makes two cocktails

5 ounces Scotch
2 teaspoons superfine sugar
16 ounces soda water
2 lemon twists

Chill two collins glasses. Pour two and a half ounces of Scotch and one teaspoon of sugar into each glass, half full of ice cubes. Fill with soda water. Stir. Garnish each with a lemon twist.

DESIGNATED DRIVER REMSEN COOLER: Chill a collins glass. Pour *1/2 an ounce of lemon juice* and *1 tablespoon of sugar* into the glass. Fill with *soda water* and ice cubes. Stir. Garnish with a *lemon twist.*

ROB ROY

makes two cocktails

4 ounces Scotch
1 ounce sweet vermouth
2 maraschino cherries

Chill two cocktail glasses. In a mixing glass, half full of ice cubes, combine all the ingredients except the maraschino cherries. Stir to mix. Strain the mixture into the glasses. Garnish each drink with a maraschino cherry.

SCOTCH MIST

makes two cocktails

4 ounces single-malt Scotch
2 lemon twists

In a cocktail shaker, half full of crushed ice, pour the single-malt Scotch. Shake gently to chill. Pour, unstrained, into two old-fashioned glasses. Garnish each drink with a wee twist of lemon.

SANGRITA

TEQUILA SUNRISE

TEQUILA SOUR

BERTHA

MARGARITA

CHIMAYO

TEQUILA

Aficionados drink their tequila straight up from a shot glass, called a shooter, with a pinch of salt and a wedge of lime (or lemon) on the side. Hot and spicy, with a killer kick on the way down, tequila complements sweet and tart partners like citrus fruits, tomatoes, pineapples, bananas, apples, coffee, and honey. Its unique dry tang makes it the perfect base for juicy cocktails such as the tequila sunrise, the tequila sour, and tequila's signature drink, the margarita. Served elegantly in a cocktail glass, garnished with a lime slice perched on the salt-coated rim, it's a tequila classic. ¶Tequila is distilled from the heart of the agave plant, a silver-blue succulent native to the Jalisco and Michoacán provinces of Mexico. Aging the clear spirit for at least two years in white oak barrels turns the color to gold and softens the biting flavor of white tequila to mellow. Either variety can be used in the recipes.

TOREADOR

makes two cocktails

3 ounces tequila
1 ounces crème de cacao
2 tablespoons heavy cream
Whipped cream

Chill two cocktail glasses. In a cocktail shaker, half full of ice cubes, combine all the ingredients except the whipped cream. Shake to mix. Strain the mixture into the glasses. Garnish each drink with a dollop of whipped cream.

CHIMAYO

makes two cocktails

3 ounces tequila
2 ounces apple juice
1 ounce crème de cassis
1 ounce lime juice

Chill two cocktail glasses. In a cocktail shaker, half full of ice cubes, combine all the ingredients. Shake to mix. Strain the mixture into the glasses.

DESIGNATED DRIVER CHIMAYO: Chill a highball glass. Pour *1 ounce of raspberry syrup* and *1/2 an ounce of lime juice* into the glass. Fill to the top with *soda water* and ice cubes. Stir gently.

BRAVE BULL

makes two cocktails

4 ounces tequila
2 ounces Kahlùa

Chill two sour glasses. In a mixing glass, half full of ice cubes, combine the ingredients. Stir to mix. Strain the mixture into the glasses.

TEQUILA SOUR

makes two cocktails

3 ounces tequila
2 ounces lemon juice
2 teaspoons confectioners' sugar

Chill two champagne flutes. In a cocktail shaker, half full of crushed ice, combine all the ingredients. Shake to mix. Strain the mixture into the glasses.

GENTLE BEN

m a k e s   t w o   c o c k t a i l s

4 ounces tequila
2 ounces vodka
2 ounces gin
6 ounces orange juice
2 teaspoons sloe gin
2 orange slices

In a blender, half full of crushed ice, combine all the ingredients except the sloe gin and orange slices. Blend at high speed for thirty seconds. Pour the mixture into two old-fashioned glasses. Float one teaspoon of sloe gin in each drink. Do not stir. Garnish with a slice of orange.

GRINGO

m a k e s   t w o   c o c k t a i l s

3 ounces tequila
1 1/2 ounces Cointreau
1 1/2 ounces brandy
3 ounces grapefruit juice

In a cocktail shaker, half full of ice cubes, combine all the ingredients. Shake to mix. Strain the mixture into two champagne flutes.

SANGRITA

m a k e s   s i x   c o c k t a i l s

5 ounces tomato juice
3 ounces orange juice
1 ounce lime juice
1 teaspoon Tabasco sauce
1 teaspoon onion juice
1 teaspoon Worcestershire sauce
Celery salt to taste
Ground white pepper to taste
9 ounces tequila

In a large pitcher, combine all the ingredients except the tequila. Stir to mix. Chill the sangrita mixture in the refrigerator for one hour. To serve the sangrita cocktails: Present each person with two shot glasses, one filled with tequila and the other filled with sangrita. Down the shot of tequila, quickly chased by the shot of sangrita.

MATADOR
makes two cocktails

3 ounces tequila
3 ounces pineapple juice
2 ounces almond syrup
1 ounce lime juice

Chill two cocktail glasses. In a mixing glass, half full of ice cubes, combine all the ingredients. Stir to mix. Strain the mixture into the glasses.

DESIGNATED DRIVER MATADOR: Chill a highball glass. Pour *3 ounces of pineapple juice, 1 ounce of almond syrup,* and *1/2 an ounce of lime juice* into the glass. Fill to the top with *soda water*. Stir gently.

MARGARITA
makes two cocktails

1 lime wedge
Coarse salt
3 ounces tequila
2 ounces lime juice
2 ounces triple sec
2 lime slices

Moisten the rims of two cocktail glasses with the lime wedge. Press the rims into a bowl of coarse salt to coat. In a cocktail shaker, half full of ice cubes, combine all the remaining ingredients except the lime slices. Shake. Strain into the glasses. Garnish each with a lime slice.

BERTHA
makes two cocktails

3 ounces tequila
1 tablespoon honey
3 ounces lime juice
16 ounces soda water

Chill two collins glasses. In a blender, half full of ice cubes, combine all the ingredients except the soda water. Blend at high speed for thirty seconds. Strain the mixture into the glasses. Fill to the top with soda water. Stir gently.

RIO GRANDE
makes two cocktails

4 ounces tequila
2 ounces Southern Comfort
2 ounces cranberry juice

Chill two cocktail glasses. In a cocktail shaker, half full of ice cubes, combine all the ingredients. Shake to mix. Strain the mixture into the glasses.

DESIGNATED DRIVER RIO GRANDE: Chill a collins glass. Pour *1/2 an ounce of lime juice* and *1 tablespoon of superfine sugar* into the glass. Fill to the top with *cranberry juice* and *ice cubes*. Stir.

LONG ISLAND ICED TEA

makes two cocktails

1 ounce tequila
1 ounce gin
1 ounce light rum
1 ounce vodka
1 ounce lemon juice
2 teaspoons superfine sugar
16 ounces cola

In a cocktail shaker, half full of ice cubes, combine all the ingredients except the cola. Shake to mix. Strain the mixture into two collins glasses, half full of ice cubes. Fill to the top with cola. Stir gently.

TEQUILA SUNRISE

makes two cocktails

3 ounces tequila
4 ounces orange juice
1/2 ounce grenadine

In a cocktail shaker, half full of ice cubes, combine the ingredients except the grenadine. Shake to mix. Strain the mixture into two collins glasses, filled with crushed ice. Float a quarter ounce of grenadine in each drink to create the "sunrise" effect. Do not stir.

MEXICAN COFFEE

makes two cocktails

3 ounces tequila
2 ounces Kahlúa
10 ounces hot coffee
Whipped cream

Warm two Irish coffee mugs. Pour one and a half ounces of tequila and one ounce of Kahlúa into each mug. Stir. Fill with hot coffee, leaving room on top for a generous dollop of whipped cream to garnish.

DESIGNATED DRIVER MEXICAN COFFEE: Warm an Irish coffee mug. Pour *1 ounce of chocolate syrup* into the mug. Fill with *hot coffee*, leaving room on top for a generous dollop of *whipped cream* to garnish.

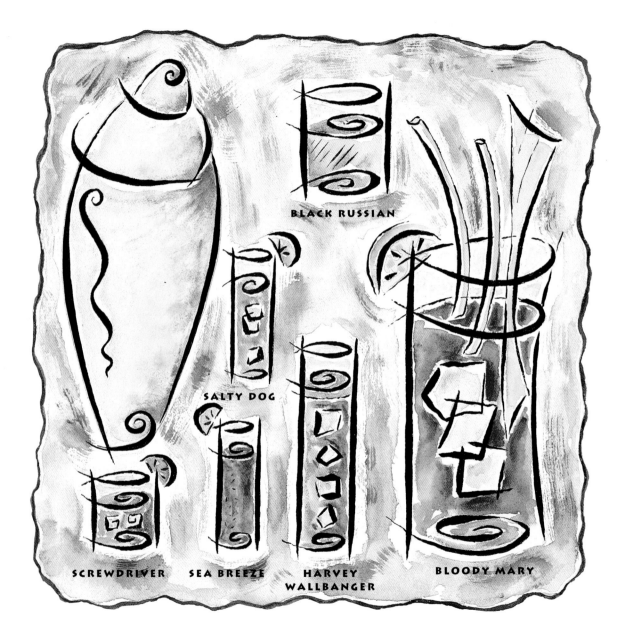

BLACK RUSSIAN

SALTY DOG

SCREWDRIVER   SEA BREEZE   HARVEY
WALLBANGER

BLOODY MARY

VODKA

Clean, crisp, and best served at glacial temperatures, vodka seems a portrait of the frigid climates that produce it: Russia, Poland, Finland, Norway, Sweden, Iceland, Canada, and a surprisingly decent contribution from northern Japan. Vodka is distilled from wheat or rye malt, then filtered through charcoal or fine sand. The ancient process of potato distillation continues to this day at small Polish breweries, but the finest vodka is grain-based. ❡Vodka is America's favorite spirit, selling millions of cases every year. Colorless, odorless, and (to the undiscerning) tasteless, vodka blends beautifully with sweet, sour, and salty flavors. The roster of drinks that enjoy vodka as their main ingredient reads like a cocktail lover's hall of fame: the screwdriver, the sea breeze, the kamikaze, and the beloved Bloody Mary. ❡The colder the vodka, the smoother the flavor. Store the bottle and a set of glasses in the freezer to serve frosty cocktails anytime.

BULLSHOT
makes two cocktails

4 ounces vodka
8 ounces beef bouillon
2 teaspoons lemon juice
1/2 teaspoon Worcestershire sauce
1/4 teaspoon Tabasco sauce

In a cocktail shaker, half full of ice cubes, combine all the ingredients. Shake to mix. Strain the mixture into two highball glasses, half full of ice cubes.

BLACK RUSSIAN
makes two cocktails

4 ounces vodka
2 ounces Kahlúa

Chill two old-fashioned glasses. Pour two ounces of vodka and one ounce of Kahlúa into each glass, half full of ice cubes. Stir to mix.

BLOODY MARY
makes two cocktails

4 ounces vodka
8 ounces tomato juice
1 ounce lemon juice
1/2 teaspoon Worcestershire sauce
1/4 teaspoon Tabasco sauce
Pinch of ground white pepper
3 pinches celery salt
2 celery stalks
2 lime slices

In a cocktail shaker, half full of ice cubes, combine all the ingredients except the celery stalks and the lime slices. Shake to mix. Strain the mixture into two highball glasses, half full of ice cubes. Garnish each drink with a celery stalk and a lime slice.

DESIGNATED DRIVER BLOODY MARY: In a cocktail shaker, a quarter full of ice cubes, combine *6 ounces of tomato juice, 1/2 an ounce of lemon juice,* a *1/4 teaspoon of Worcestershire sauce, 1 dash of Tabasco,* and pinches of *white pepper* and *celery salt.* Shake to mix. Strain into a highball glass, half full of ice cubes. Garnish with a celery stalk and a lime slice.

CAPE CODDER

makes two cocktails

4 ounces vodka
10 ounces cranberry juice
2 lime wedges

Chill two highball glasses. Pour two ounces of vodka and five ounces of cranberry juice into each glass, half full of ice cubes. Stir. Garnish each with a lime wedge. **DESIGNATED DRIVER CAPE CODDER:** Chill a highball glass. Pour *4 ounces of cranberry juice* into the glass. Fill to the top with *soda water* and ice cubes. Stir gently. Garnish with a *lime wedge.*

GREYHOUND

makes two cocktails

4 ounces vodka
10 ounces grapefruit juice

Chill two highball glasses. Pour two ounces of vodka and five ounces of grapefruit juice into each glass, half full of ice cubes. Stir to mix.

CHI CHI

makes two cocktails

4 ounces vodka
10 ounces pineapple juice
2 ounces coconut cream
2 maraschino cherries
2 pineapple slices

In a blender, half full of crushed ice, combine all the ingredients except the maraschino cherries and the pineapple slices. Blend at high speed for thirty seconds. Pour the mixture into two collins glasses. Garnish each drink with a maraschino cherry and a pineapple slice. **DESIGNATED DRIVER CHI CHI:** In a blender, a quarter full of crushed ice, combine *6 ounces of pineapple juice* and *1 ounce of coconut cream.* Blend at high speed for thirty seconds. Pour the mixture into a collins glass, half full of ice cubes. Garnish with a *maraschino cherry* and a *pineapple slice.*

FUZZY NAVEL

2 ounces vodka
2 ounces peach schnapps
12 ounces orange juice

Chill two collins glasses. Pour one ounce of vodka, one ounce of peach schnapps, and six ounces of orange juice into each glass, half full of ice cubes. Stir.

DESIGNATED DRIVER FUZZY NAVEL: Chill a collins glass. Pour *6 ounces of peach nectar* and *4 ounces of orange juice* into the glass, half full of ice cubes. Stir.

HARVEY WALLBANGER

3 ounces vodka
8 ounces orange juice
1 ounce Galliano

Chill two highball glasses. Pour one and a half ounces of vodka and four ounces of orange juice into each glass, half full of ice cubes. Stir to mix. Float half an ounce of Galliano in each drink. Do not stir.

HARLEM COCKTAIL

3 ounces vodka
2 ounces pineapple juice
2 teaspoons maraschino liqueur
4 small pineapple slices

Chill two cocktail glasses. In a cocktail shaker, half full of ice cubes, combine all the ingredients except the pineapple slices. Shake to mix. Strain the mixture into the glasses. Garnish each drink with two pineapple slices, speared on a toothpick.

DESIGNATED DRIVER HARLEM COCKTAIL: Chill a cocktail glass. In a cocktail shaker, a quarter full of ice cubes, combine *1 ounce of cherry juice* and *2 ounces of pineapple juice*. Shake to mix. Strain the mixture into the glass. Garnish with *2 pineapple slices,* speared on a toothpick.

SALTY DOG
m a k e s   t w o   c o c k t a i l s

1 lime wedge
Coarse salt
4 ounces vodka
10 ounces grapefruit juice

Moisten the rims of two highball glasses with the lime wedge. Press the rims into a bowl of coarse salt to coat. In a cocktail shaker, half full of ice cubes, combine all the remaining ingredients. Shake to mix. Strain the mixture into the glasses, half full of ice cubes.

KAMIKAZE
m a k e s   t w o   c o c k t a i l s

2 ounces vodka
2 ounces triple sec
2 ounces lime juice

In a mixing glass, half full of ice cubes, combine all the ingredients. Stir to mix. Strain the mixture into two cocktail glasses.

SEA BREEZE
m a k e s   t w o   c o c k t a i l s

4 ounces vodka
6 ounces cranberry juice
6 ounces grapefruit juice
2 lemon wedges

Chill two highball glasses. In a cocktail shaker, half full of ice cubes, combine all the ingredients except the lemon wedges. Shake to mix. Strain the mixture into the glasses, half full of crushed ice. Garnish each drink with a lemon wedge.

DESIGNATED DRIVER SEA BREEZE: Chill a highball glass. In a cocktail shaker, half full of ice cubes, combine *4 ounces of cranberry juice* and *4 ounces of grapefruit juice*. Shake to mix. Strain the mixture into the glass, half full of crushed ice. Garnish with a *lemon wedge*.

SEX ON THE BEACH

makes two cocktails

2 ounces vodka
2 ounces peach schnapps
4 ounces pineapple juice
4 ounces cranberry juice
2 teaspoons coconut cream

Chill two highball glasses. Pour one ounce of vodka, one ounce of peach schnapps, two ounces of pineapple juice, two ounces of cranberry juice, and one teaspoon of coconut cream into each glass, half full of ice cubes. Stir to mix.

DESIGNATED DRIVER SEX ON THE BEACH: Chill a highball glass. Pour *2 ounces of peach nectar, 3 ounces of pineapple juice, 3 ounces of cranberry juice,* and *1 teaspoon of coconut cream* into the glass, half full of ice cubes. Stir to mix.

SCREWDRIVER

makes two cocktails

4 ounces vodka
10 ounces orange juice
2 orange slices

Chill two old-fashioned glasses. Pour two ounces of vodka and five ounces of orange juice into each glass, half full of ice cubes. Stir to mix. Garnish each drink with an orange slice.

WOO WOO

makes two cocktails

3 ounces vodka
1 ounce peach schnapps
6 ounces cranberry juice

Chill two old-fashioned glasses. Pour one and a half ounces of vodka, half an ounce of peach schnapps, and three ounces of cranberry juice into each glass, half full of ice cubes. Stir to mix.

DESIGNATED DRIVER WOO WOO: Chill a sour glass. Pour *2 ounces of peach nectar* and *4 ounces of cranberry juice* into the glass. Stir.

WHISKEY

The word whiskey comes from the Gaelic phrase for "water of life," and is the family name for spirits distilled from grains. The type, combination, and maturation process of the grain or grains give the individual whiskey its distinct flavor and texture. ¶The whiskey cocktail recipes are divided into three groups: American blended whiskey, bourbon, and Irish whiskey. Balanced American blended whiskey mixes classic Manhattans, old-fashioneds, and whiskey sours. Spirited bourbon, distilled from corn and never blended, puts the bite in a refreshing mint julep and the sting in a Pernod-soaked Sazerac. Smoky Irish whiskey stirs a chest-warming Irish coffee cocktail. (Don't forget the dollop of whipped cream!) ¶Stalwart whiskey makes a grand statement mixed with sweet liqueurs, tangy fruits, and aromatic herbs, flavors that hold their own beside its big taste.

ST. PATRICK'S DAY COCKTAIL

OLD-FASHIONED

MINT JULEP   IRISH COFFEE   SAZERAC   MANHATTAN

WINE

Sparkling or still, red or white, wine cocktails are low in alcohol content, light in taste, and long on flavor — excellent for any occasion. Blend wine with sweet vermouth, fruity liqueurs, or stinging bitters to put the punch in your punch. Serve sangría, the tart and tempting fruit-spiked red wine *refresco* from Spain. Toss a sugar cube into a chilled flute filled with the bubbly for a simple, simply delicious champagne cocktail. Or, pair champagne with a peach for elegance. There are many marvelous concoctions to create with wine as the base: you needn't wait for a party to sample them. ¶*In vino veritas*, however, the flavor of the best Bordeaux or French Champagne is masked in a mixed drink. Save money without sacrificing taste and use domestic champagnes, sparkling white wines, or dry red and white table wines to substitute for pricey foreign fare — and let the festivities begin.

CHAMPAGNE CUP

ADONIS

CHAMPAGNE COCKTAIL

SANGRIA

CHAMPAGNE COOLER

makes two cocktails

2 ounces brandy
2 ounces triple sec
8 ounces chilled champagne
2 mint sprigs

Chill two white wineglasses. Pour one ounce of brandy and one ounce of triple sec into each glass. Fill to the top with chilled champagne. Stir gently. Garnish each drink with a sprig of mint.

BELLINI

makes two cocktails

8 ounces chilled champagne
4 ounces peach nectar

Chill two champagne flutes. In a mixing glass, combine the ingredients. Stir gently. Pour the mixture into the flutes.

DESIGNATED DRIVER BELLINI: Chill a champagne flute. Pour *2 ounces of peach nectar* into the flute. Fill to the top with *chilled sparkling apple cider*. Stir gently.

CHAMPAGNE COCKTAIL

makes two cocktails

2 sugar cubes
4 dashes bitters
12 ounces chilled champagne
2 candied violets

Chill two champagne flutes. Place a sugar cube in the bottom of each flute. Drop two dashes of bitters on each sugar cube. Fill the flutes to the top with chilled champagne. Do not stir. Garnish each drink with a candied violet.

DESIGNATED DRIVER CHAMPAGNE COCKTAIL: Chill a champagne flute. Place a *sugar cube* in the bottom of the flute. Drop *2 dashes of bitters* on the sugar cube. Fill the flute to the top with *chilled sparkling apple cider*. Do not stir. Garnish with a *candied violet.*

KIR ROYALE

m a k e s   t w o   c o c k t a i l s

1 ounce crème de cassis
12 ounces chilled champagne
2 lemon twists

Chill two champagne flutes. Pour half an ounce of crème de cassis into each flute. Fill to the top with chilled champagne. Stir gently. Garnish each drink with a lemon twist.

DESIGNATED DRIVER KIR ROYALE: Chill a champagne flute. Pour *1/2 an ounce of black currant syrup* into the flute. Fill to the top with *chilled sparkling apple cider.* Stir gently. Garnish with a *lemon twist.*

MIMOSA

m a k e s   t w o   c o c k t a i l s

1 ounce Cointreau
6 ounces orange juice
12 ounces chilled champagne

Pour half an ounce of Cointreau and three ounces of orange juice into two red wineglasses. Fill to the top with chilled champagne. Stir gently.

DESIGNATED DRIVER MIMOSA: Chill a red wineglass. Pour *3 ounces of orange juice* into the wineglass. Fill to the top with *chilled sparkling apple cider.* Stir gently.

CHAMPAGNE CUP

m a k e s   s i x   c o c k t a i l s

20 ounces chilled champagne
3 1/2 ounces brandy
2 ounces Curaçao
1 ounce maraschino liqueur
1 ounce Grand Marnier
6 orange slices
6 pineapple slices
6 mint sprigs

In a punch bowl, a quarter full of ice cubes, combine all the ingredients except the fruit and mint. Stir. Garnish with sliced fruit and mint sprigs. Serve in punch cups.

BLACK VELVET

m a k e s   t w o   c o c k t a i l s

8 ounces chilled champagne
12 ounces stout

Chill two collins glasses. Pour four ounces of chilled champagne into each glass. Add six ounces of stout to each drink, pouring slowly. Stir gently to mix.

ADONIS COCKTAIL

makes two cocktails

4 ounces dry sherry
2 ounces sweet vermouth
2 dashes orange bitters
2 orange twists

Chill two cocktail glasses. In a mixing glass, half full of ice cubes, combine all the ingredients except the orange twists. Stir to mix. Strain the mixture into the glasses. Garnish each drink with an orange twist.

BISHOP

makes two cocktails

6 ounces full-bodied red wine
2 ounces lemon juice
3 ounces orange juice
2 teaspoons superfine sugar
2 orange slices

In a cocktail shaker, half full of ice cubes, combine all the ingredients except the orange slices. Shake to mix. Strain the mixture into two highball glasses, half full of ice cubes. Garnish each drink with an orange slice.

SANGRÍA

makes six cocktails

32 ounces dry red wine
2 ounces brandy
3 ounces triple sec
8 ounces orange juice
4 ounces lemon juice
8 ounces soda water
4 orange slices
4 lime slices
4 lemon slices

In a large pitcher, a quarter full of ice cubes, combine all the ingredients. Stir. Serve in red wineglasses.

WHITE WINE SPRITZER

makes two cocktails

8 ounces dry white wine
12 ounces soda water
2 lime twists

Pour four ounces of white wine into two collins glasses, half full of ice cubes. Fill with soda water. Stir gently. Garnish each drink with a twist of lime.

DESIGNATED DRIVER WHITE WINE SPRITZER: Chill a collins glass. Pour *1/2 an ounce of lime juice* and *1 tablespoon of sugar* into the glass. Fill to the top with *soda water* and *ice cubes*. Stir. Garnish with a *lime twist*.

RASPBERRY COCKTAIL

makes two cocktails

1 cup fresh raspberries
4 ounces gin
8 ounces full-bodied white wine
4 ounces kirsch

Chill two red wineglasses. In a small glass bowl, combine the raspberries and the gin. Marinate for one hour. In a blender, half full of ice cubes, combine the raspberry-gin mixture, the white wine, and the kirsch. Blend at high speed for thirty seconds. Strain the mixture into the glasses.

DESIGNATED DRIVER RASPBERRY COCKTAIL: Chill a red wineglass. Pour *1 ounce of raspberry syrup* into the glass. Fill to the top with *soda water.* Stir gently. Garnish with *3 fresh raspberries.*

GLÖGG

makes two cocktails

12 ounces dry red wine
3 ounces brandy
2 whole cloves
1 cardamon pod, crushed
1 cinnamon stick
1 tablespoon raisins
1 tablespoon blanched almonds
1 1/2 tablespoons granulated sugar
1 teaspoon brown sugar

Warm two Irish coffee mugs. In a nonreactive saucepan, combine all the ingredients except the brown sugar. Stir over medium heat to dissolve the granulated sugar. Just before the boiling point, very carefully ignite the surface of the mixture with a long matchstick. Quickly and carefully, sprinkle the brown sugar into the flames. Allow the flames to burn for ten seconds, then cover the pan to extinguish the fire. Remove a spoonful of raisins and almonds to place in the bottom of each mug. Pour the glögg into the mugs.

Index

Cocktails listed with boldface page numbers have Designated Driver versions.